HABIT STACKING

Introduce Small Habits into Your Routine to Beat Procrastination and Double Your Output

BOOK DESCRIPTION

This book is a daily companion that enables you to easily and practically apply a good set of habits in small, yet powerful doses into your routine. This is so you can overcome procrastination and eventually double your output.

The book starts off by helping you lay the foundation of your habit stacks. In this regard, it employs a beginners' approach by synthesizing for you what habit stacking entails. With this foundation, it goes further by proposing to you great habits that you should implement and the order in which you ought to implement them.

Lack of a practical hands-on approach is what dissuades many from overcoming bad habits and entrenching good habits into their own daily lives. This book provides you with practical hands-on step-by-step instructions on how to create a simple, memorable yet powerful habit stack that would not only keep procrastination at bay but also optimize your productivity in all areas of your life.

Having provided you with crisp-clear knowledge of habit stacking and highly effective step-by-step instructions on how to create simple yet powerful habit stacks, the books navigates you to greater depths into the core domains of your life – home, health, relationships, finances and business. It helps you create a blueprint stack for each of these core domains. A blueprint that you can easily expand and customize to suit your very own unique individual needs.

Kill the bad habits! This is your book. Seize it. Read it.

Enjoy your reading.

GIFT INCLUDED

If you are an entrepreneur, an aspiring entrepreneur, someone who is trying to create additional income stream, or even someone who just loves self improvement books; then you need to read my recommendations for top 10 business books ever.

ABOUT THE AUTHOR

George Pain is an entrepreneur, author and business consultant. He specializes in setting up online businesses from scratch, investment income strategies and global mobility solutions. He has built several businesses from the ground up, and is excited to share his knowledge with readers.

DISCLAIMER

Copyright © 2017

All Rights Reserved

No part of this book can be transmitted or reproduced in any form including print, electronic, photocopying, scanning, mechanical or recording without prior written permission from the author.

While the author has taken the utmost effort to ensure the accuracy of the written content, all readers are advised to follow information mentioned herein at their own risk. The author cannot be held responsible for any personal or commercial damage caused by information. All readers are encouraged to seek professional advice when needed.

CONTENTS

HABIT STACKING 1

BOOK DESCRIPTION 3

GIFT INCLUDED 5

ABOUT THE AUTHOR 6

DISCLAIMER 7

CONTENTS 8

INTRODUCTION 10

WHAT IS HABIT STACKING? 12

WHAT CAUSES GOOD AND BAD HABITS? 24

HOW TO CREATE A HABIT STACK 36

HABIT STACKING FOR HOME LIFE 46

HABIT STACKING FOR HEALTH 54

HABIT STACK FOR RELATIONSHIPS 61

HABIT STACKS FOR FINANCES 69

HABIT STACKS FOR BUSINESS 76

CONCLUSION 84

INTRODUCTION

There is nothing that stinks like bad habits. Yet, just like me, I wouldn't expect you to feel happy when someone bluntly shouts at you 'YOU STINK!...' in front of your family, loved ones, friends, peers and seniors. Yet, unfortunately, BAD HABITS SHOUT OUT LOUD!

Bad habits have a way of deafening your ears so that you don't get to hear your very own internal voice shouting out that you stink. Luckily, this book, "Habit Stacking: Introduce Small Habits into Your Routine to Beat Procrastination and Double Your Output" is there for you.

This book is a soft voice of reason that not only respectively and privately helps you to identify your bad habits, but also, gives you a good set of habits that you can use to replace your bad habits. It has simplified this set of good habits into habit stacks – each stack covering a core domain of your life - home, health, relationships, finance and business.

With this daily companion, you are able to transform yourself, stop procrastination and optimize your productivity. The benefits are too immense to condense into this small book. Yet, health, wealth, satisfaction, joy and happiness are ultimately within your reach.

Keep reading!

WHAT IS HABIT STACKING?

Life would be so tedious if we did not have habits and routines in our lives. We would all be starting anew each and every day, and, probably, each and every moment. Today would end without us having achieved much, but, unknowingly repeating what we did yesterday. Things that, more often than not, we do subconsciously and almost spontaneously would not happen. Thus, habits are important to our everyday lives.

Habit stacking has become one of the best ways by which we can enhance our habits to stop procrastination and increase our output. But, before we go farther into the depth of habit stacking, let's remind ourselves what stacking is all about. We need also to remind ourselves what habits are all about and their importance in our daily lives.

What is Stacking?

Stacking is the process of creating stacks. A stack is simply a pile of things arranged in a neat order. These things could be objects, subjects, actions, etc.

Thus, stacking is the systematic orderly arrangement of things.

What is habit?

A habit is a repetitive pattern of doing things.

How are habits formed?

Habit formation is the way by which a behavior, through repetition, becomes habitual or automatic. The following is a three-step process known as the habit-loop by which habit formation goes through;

1. Trigger (cue)
2. Routine
3. Reward

What is a cue?

A cue is simply a signal that triggers an occurence.

A trigger or cue informs your brain to go into automatic mode and let your behavior unfold.

What is routine?

A routine is a repetitive sequence of events/actions regularly followed when a cue is triggered. Common routines include waking up, going to bathe, taking breakfast and going to school/work.

Most of our daily lives follow routines. For example, at work, we have a daily reporting and departing routine, in addition to lunch-time routine.

Why routine?

The following are the key benefits of routine;

1. A routine helps to make it quicker to do repetitive tasks.

2. A routine ensures thoroughness as some tasks and activities that would have otherwise been forgotten are remembered.

3. Routine helps to quantify performance.

4. Routine boosts productivity as each repetition improves performance rate.

5. Routine enables easy evaluation and control measures to be put in place.

What is a reward?

A reward is any inducement advanced towards positive affirmation of a given outcome. It is the positive gain or a like by the brain that makes it remember a particular habit loop.

Reward can be;

- Monetary – Wage, salary, commission, rent, etc.

- Physical – A kiss, a hug, sexual intercourse, etc.

- Mental – A score in an exam, etc.

- Psychological – Motivation, satisfaction, etc.

- Emotional – Friendship, comradeship, mentorship, affection, etc.

- Spiritual – Joy, happiness, peace, serenity, etc.

- A combination of some or all of the above

Why reward?

A reward helps to reinforce good outcomes. It helps to reinforce good deeds into good habits.

What is habit stacking?

Habit stacking refers to the systematic orderly arrangement of habits in such a manner that allows each habit to be easily recalled and executed in the most optimal way.

Why habit stacking?

Habit stacking groups similar habits in such a manner that makes them easily remembered and executed as a group.

Criteria for creating a habit stack

In order to create a habit stack, the following criteria is required;

1. Time – Time is of utmost importance. At what time is a habit going to be executed?

2. Sequence – A habit stack is procedural. It must have a defined sequence of moving from one habit to the next.

3. Spontaneity – a habit stack should have an element of spontaneity. That is, it should be capable of being partially or wholly self-executing

4. Tasking – a habit stack should allow easy tasking of work. Ideally (but not always practical), a habit stack should form a task.

Why Habit Stacking?

Habit stacking serves the following benefits;

1. It is easy to remember of a set of habits to be executed.

2. It allows for quick execution of tasks.

3. It reduces energy expended by brain in thinking.

4. It results in optimal productivity.

Can Habit Stacking be nested?

Yes, habit stacking can be nested. This is simply because, most of the day, you perform different routines in sequential order. Yet, these routines are hardly for the same task. For example, while at home, you can still carry out preparatory tasks for your workplace or study place. While at home, you can revise your lesson or work schedule so as to know which books to carry with you or which attire to wear for your day's work.

Some habits such as relationship habits have to be carried out wherever you are - be it at home, school, work, gym or elsewhere. Health habits, such as mobility fitness exercises, can also be carried out wherever you are. They will certainly have to be nested or interspersed within other habit stacks.

Thus, **nested habit stacks** are more of a norm than an exception.

How are habits wired in the brain?

Habits are formed in the brain circuitry through a synaptic process. In neurology, a synapse is a connection between two brain neurons. When two neurons are fired (activated) together, they form a synapse. A synapse has been known to play a big part in memory formation. Thus, every firing of a pair of neurons results in a certain memory code (such as a 'bit' in computer science). Several pairs of neurons may need to be fired together to form a complete memory (about a certain piece of information such as relating to a particular habit). The more frequent this firing occurs the more the circuit gets etched, smoothened out and perfected.

Are there good and bad habits?

Yes, there exist good habits just as there are bad habits. Habits are intentioned to simplify our lives by automatic routines so that the brain is left free to think about non-routine and creative functions.

Good habits are those that simplify and make your life easier and better. However, bad habits are those that simplify the process of making your life more difficult and much worse.

What determines a good versus bad habit?

Sometimes, it is difficult for one to distinguish between a good habit and a bad habit. It at times occurs that one person's bad habit is another person's good habit and vice versa. So, what is the distinguishing line?

Well, knowing what a good habit is and what a bad habit is will help you draw a distinctive line between the two and thus help you classify your habits as good or bad;

- Good habits propel you to achieve your goal or destination; whether it's to finish your project on time, lose weight, be healthy, make more money or simply be happy.

- Bad habits, on the other hand, slow you down, hinder you, stop you, block you, or eventually prevent you from attaining your goal or arriving at your destination.

Why are habits important?

The importance of habits cannot be overemphasized. There are many great benefits of good habits. Good habits:

- Help to make your work easier by establishing repetitive patterns which are mastered and reinforced each and every time you repeat them.

- Make it easier for you to establish benchmarks that you can easily use to evaluate each and every step you undertake in dealing with issues; thus making analysis, feedback, control and decision making more accurate and precise.

- Help to bring predictability in each and every endeavor you make since others and you can easily interpret the habitual patterns with greater certainty and precision.

- Help to strengthen your character and contributes towards building a better personality.

- Enable you to have faith, win trust and build long-lasting and beneficial relationships.

- Boosts your overall wellbeing thus enabling you to live longer, healthier and happier

The Power of Habit

Habits are the most potent part of your arsenal. However, like any other arsenal, it all depends how you go about using it. If you point the arsenal against you, it will kill you. But if you point it against that which threatens your very existence, then, you are likely going to live another day.

Bad habits are dangerous. They ruin your life. They make you fail to achieve your full potential. They seep out energy from you. They leave you worn out, tired, poor, feeble and unhappy. Bad habits shorten your lifespan. Bad habits do kill, albeit in thousands of unknowing ways.

The antidote to bad habits is good habits. Nurture good habits. And like pouring water into a cup full of oil, drip by drip, oil will flow out being displaced by every drop of water that enters the cup. In the long-run, the cup will be full of water and free from oil. This is what happens when you drop-by-drop fill your tank of habits with good habits. Bad habits will naturally get out.

Habits help you do routines less strenuously, less laboriously thus sparing your mental resources towards creative endeavors. The more you cultivate good habits in your life, the less stressed you become since your conscious mindset is freed towards creative applications that help you achieve your highest aspirations.

Dangers of Bad Habits

Bad habits just do the opposite of good habits. Bad habits:

- Make you sacrifice more than necessary in achieving your goals, if indeed you achieve them.

- Destroy your character and personality leaving you as someone to be shunned and avoided by right-thinking members of society.

- Kill good relationships leaving you with no choice but attract bad relationships that serve to destroy you even more

- Make you lose faith, lose trust and end up with non-beneficial relationships.

- Bring pain, suffering, poor health, lack of happiness and shorter miserable lifespan.

Quick tips to end bad habits

The following are important tips that psychologists agree will help you not only succeed in killing your bad habits but also enhance good habits:

1. Acknowledge your bad habits.
2. Gather sufficient knowledge about your bad habits.
3. Understand that your bad habits can be changed.
4. Learn what you need to do in order to confront your bad habits.
5. Prepare a habit goal for you to confront your bad habits.
6. Establish measurable and attainable habit stacks.
7. Calibrate your stacks into attainable routines.
8. Devise appropriate feedback and control measures to guide and determine your performance as you embark on each routine.
9. Meticulously execute your habit stacks.

10. Measure your performance and take appropriate control measures.

11. Do celebrate after each and every success.

WHAT CAUSES GOOD AND BAD HABITS?

It is obvious that you should implement good habits. Yet, before we dwell on the good habits, let's explore the causes of both the good and bad habits so that we can be better decide how to implement each to have the most optimal impact.

What brings about good habits?

Sometimes to understand good habits, it is important to first know what brings them about. The following are some of the factors that bring about or contribute to good habits;

- **Genetics** – Scientific studies have indicated that certain habits are shaped by genetic factors. For example, various studies have shown that there are certain genes that predispose men to marital fidelity. There are also certain genes that predispose some people to good temper, emotional stability and boldness. These brings about certain habits such as habits of non-violence, habits of marital fidelity and habits of sticking to saying truth and doing that which is right no matter the consequences.

- **Culture** – We all belong to cultures. Culture plays a very big role in shaping one's worldviews. Norms and standards are all products of culture and vary from one society to another. Norms and standards of one culture may breed habits that appear to be good to that culture yet become abominable in another culture. For example, while the Western society accepts and tolerates the habit of homosexuality, in African culture this is held as abominable. On the other hand, while African society accepts and tolerates the habit of polygamy, in Western society this is abominable.

- **Upbringing** – Parents are the first teachers of a child. A child learns between good and bad habits from parents. When a certain habit is condemned by a parent, a child knows that this is a bad habit. On the other hand, when a certain habit is condoned by a parent, a child considers this habit as good. Apart from parents, schools and religious institutions greatly contributes to shaping good habits in young ones.

- **Peer influence** – Beyond families, children and youth learn so much about good habits from their friends. Peer pressure can cause them to even dissociate themselves from the good habits they were taught by their parents and thus embrace the bad habits that they do consider good from their peers. However, peer influence too can bring good habits, especially if it emanates from a good peer group. That is why it is important to take into consideration the qualities of the people you choose to associate with as your peers.

While we cannot change our genetic composition, we can overcome some of its negative consequences such as bad habits by learning to take control of them. Other than genetic factors, all the other factors are simply factors that we have learned. Just as we have learned them we too can unlearn them.

What causes bad habits?

There are suggestions that are more often floated around as to the real causes of bad habits. We have seen genetics, upbringing, peer influence as some of the contributing factors to good habits. These too can be contributing factors to bad habits in terms of adverse effects. However, most psychologists concur that the following are major causes of bad habits:

1. Depleted willpower
2. Innate human defiance
3. Need for social acceptance
4. Inability to truly understand the nature of risk
5. Inability to rationalize unhealthy habits
6. Genetic predisposition to addiction

Depleted willpower

Willpower is the most omnipotent word when it comes to killing a bad habit. It is the orbit that other methods and strategies revolve around and without which the center cannot hold.

Willpower is that force that urges you to actualize your will. It keeps you focused on asserting your determined will regardless of the swaying from others, be it persuasive or coercive.

Depleted willpower is caused by:

- Scarcity – Perpetual scarcity makes it easy for people to lose their willpower. For example, those who wish to have a balanced diet may give up on their willpower if inadequate supplies of fruits and vegetables become perpetual.

- Money troubles - Studies find that money troubles have strong negative psychological effect on the poor. Money troubles impair their thought-process as they slowly adapt to conditions that requires less willpower to overcome. For example, it is a bad habit to pick from dumpsites, but money troubles may cause the poor to do that not because they know it is a bad habit, but their willpower has been lowered by money troubles.

- Constant decision-making – When people encounter many scenarios that require quick and constant decision-making, their mind gets worked-up and soon their willpower to continue making more decisions gets impaired.

- Stress – Stress is as a result of overworked mental energy. Willpower consumes energy. Thus, when you are stressed, there is less energy available to your willpower.

Innate human defiance

Human beings are by nature defiant. This is not a bad natural phenomenon as such as it is necessary for human beings to be adventurous and discover new things. For example, youth learn to become defiant of excessive parental control which is necessary for them to establish their own self-control as grown-up adults; some employees become defiant of perpetually being employed which is necessary for them create their own enterprises; slaves defy their masters against perpetual slavery which is necessary for them to become free. However, if this innate human defiance is not put into proper perspective and proper use (for example, when a child defies a parent's proper instructions without being reprimanded) it can lead to bad habits.

Need for social acceptance

Human beings are social beings by nature, thus, peer pressure and at times a need to conform to traditions may lead to bad habits. Peer pressure is strongest amongst adolescents and thus bad habit may be acquired from one adolescent to the other.

Inability to truly understand the nature of risk

Some people engage in bad habits such as drug and alcohol abuse due to lack of proper understanding and appreciation of the magnitude of risk involved such as suicide, mental illness, cancer and other health and social risks.

Inability to rationalize healthy habits

Some people are unable to rationalize healthy habits (for example the need to take alcohol in moderation, avoid food bingeing, avoid smoking, etc) thus making them engage recklessly in irrational habits such as drug addiction, bingeing, cigarette smoking, etc.

Genetic predisposition to addiction

Scientists have proven that there are certain genes that predispose some people to engage in bad habits. For example, adultery, infidelity and promiscuity are some of the bad sexual habits. Studies have found that there some genes contribute to these bad habits.

How do you tell that certain habits are good for you?

The following are telling signs that a certain habit is good for you;

- If the habit makes you more fit for work, study or exercise (e.g. waking up early).
- If the habit leads to your seniors, colleagues and peers complimenting you
- If the habit makes you feel energized, motivated and willing to do good things.
- If the habit leads you to feeling less burdened.
- If the habit makes you fill accomplished, satisfied and happy.
- If the habit makes you get embraced by people who are respected and highly regarded within your community.

How do you tell that certain habits are bad for you?

The following are some characteristics that can help you tell that a certain habit is bad for you:

- If the habit makes you feel unfit to do anything positive in your life such as exercising, working, studying, etc.

- If the habit gets you reprimanded or receive negative feedback from your seniors, colleagues and peers.

- If the habit makes you feel withdrawn, depleted off energy and willpower, lack motivation and unwillingness to do good things.

- If the habit makes you feel bitterness, regret, and increases willingness to do harm either to yourself or others.

- If the habit makes you feel overburdened or worn-out.

- If the habit makes you feel un-accomplished, unsatisfied and unhappy.

- If the habit makes you get avoided or shunned by right-thinking members of your community, especially those who are held as respectable, good-mannered and noble.

Bad habits have consequences. The following are the negative consequences of bad habits.

1. Poor personality.
2. Poor family relationships.
3. Poor academic endeavors.

4. Poor work output.
5. Poor social relationships.
6. Poor leadership.
7. Poor health.

Poor personality

Poor personality is that personality that doesn't fully manifest the best of you as you are capable of being, but rather, manifests the character that you acquired and which you ought not to have.

Poor family relationship

The greatest ingredient leading to family feuds and breakups are bad habits. Bad financial habits that deny the family essential resources, bad habits of drug and alcohol addiction that lead to domestic violence and failure of a spouse to fulfill his/her conjugal obligations, bad habits that cause children not to respect their parents and vice versa are well known to contribute to poor family relationship.

Poor academic endeavors

Bad habits at school such as plagiarism, bullying, stealing, etc, impair learning. An impaired learning yields poor academic performance and thus greatly hampers one's academic endeavors.

Poor work output

Bad habits at work such as lateness, moonlighting, avoiding work, etc, negate one's productivity and thus contribute to poor work output which may constrain career progression and at worst constrain one's income flows due to reprimands, suspensions and sackings.

Poor relationship with others

Bad relationship habits such as jealousy, complaining, gossiping, etc, lead to relationship challenges such as fighting, arguing, and if in marriage, divorce.

Poor leadership

Poor leadership is one of the greatest challenges of the modern era. As human organizations become more complex and as human beings continue to increasingly depend on organizations, poor leadership becomes a great endemic. It not only affects families, it affects communities, organizations, societies and nations. Poor leadership has caused almost all of the wars ever known in history leading to catastrophes that have claimed hundreds of millions of people's lives.

In what order should you implement your good habits?

Good habits are many. You need so many good habits to implement on a daily basis. Thus, listing them here would be quite tedious for you to master. Nonetheless, this book introduces habit stacking as a way by which you can orderly implement good habits.

Subsequent Sections in this book will dwell on these stacks. In a nutshell, the following are stacks containing habits that you should implement which will later on be discussed in details;

1. **Habit stacks for Business** – Contains a set of habits you need to implement on daily basis so as to have business success.

2. **Habit stack for home life** – Has habits that you can easily implement in order to have a happy, stress-free homely life.

3. **Habit stack for relationships** – Has powerful set of habits that will re-invigorate your relationships and strengthen your relationship bond with your spouse, family members, friends, peers, colleagues and your superiors.

4. **Habit stack for health** – These are simple habits that you can apply on daily basis and will will help you avoid

infections, stop pre-mature aging, be strong and live longer.

5. **Habit stack for finances** – This is a set of habits that will help you not only gain financial independence but also make sound investments and grow your wealth.

A Short message from the Author:

Hey, are you enjoying the book? I'd love to hear your thoughts!

Many readers do not know how hard reviews are to come by, and how much they help an author.

I would be incredibly thankful if you could take just 60 seconds to write a brief review on Amazon, even if it's just a few sentences!

Please head to the product page, and leave a review as shown below.

Thank you for taking the time to share your thoughts! Your review will genuinely make a difference for me and help gain exposure for my work.

HOW TO CREATE A HABIT STACK

We have so many good habits that we need to reinforce in our lives. We too have so many bad habits we need to kill in our lives. They can seem overwhelming. However, creating stack for each category makes the work much easier.

The following are steps for creating a stack:

1. Determine the core areas of your life that needs habit transformation
2. Create a stack for each of these core areas
3. List bad habits to kill for each stack
4. List good habits (including those needed to kill bad habits) for each stack
5. Prioritize good habits for each of stack
6. Create a stack loop.
7. If possible, create a routine loop for each habit within the stack

Step 1: Determine the core areas of your life that needs habit transformation

What are the core areas of your life that needs habit transformation?

This is a question that is specific to each individual. Each individual has unique habitual needs. Nonetheless, in this book, we will take a general approach that is applicable to all.

The following are the 5 core areas for consideration; business, home life, relationships, health and finance.

Step 2: Creating a stack for each core area

After identifying our 5 core areas of life that needs habit transformation, we can now create a stack for each. The following are our 5 stacks;

1. Habit stack for business
2. Habit stack for home life
3. Habit stack for relationships
4. Habit stack for health
5. Habit stack for finances

In what order should these stacks be implemented?

As the adage goes, charity begins at home. Before we go to work, studies, hospital (when we are sick) it all begins at home. Also, the first and the most enduring relationships begin at home, and, probably, end at home (in marriage, etc). Only after having good home life habits can we be healthy.

With good home life habits and health habits, our relationship both at home and outside home begins to develop and grow. Relationships are what help to create business. Business is nothing but a service offered through relationship networks. Good relationship habits strengthen business.

Finance is what funds your lifestyle. You need finance to fund your education and that of your family. You need finance to buy a home. You need finance to start a business. Good finance habits will help you realize your goals.

Thus, the best way to implement these stacks is to begin with;

1. Home life
2. Health
3. Relationships
4. Finance
5. Business

Hence, we will re-arrange our stacks in this book to flow along the above order.

Step 3: List bad habits to substitute for each stack

Bad habits are many and varied. The best way to expose them is to classify them. The following is a simple and basic classification of them:

1. Bad habits at home

2. Bad health habits
3. Bad habits in relationships
4. Bad finance habits
5. Bad business habits

Step 4: List good habits for each stack

In this step, list those good habits, most importantly, those good habits that you need in order to counter the bad habits you already have.

Just as in bad habits, good habits will be categorized the same way;

1. Good habits at home
2. Good health habits
3. Good habits in relationships
4. Good finance habits
5. Good business habits

Step 5: Prioritize good habits for each of stack

There are those habits that are primary, overriding, initiating or of utmost importance for others to succeed. Start with them in the order of priority.

Step 6: Create a stack loop

Just as we have a habit loop, create a stack loop with the very same components. That is;

- Cue/trigger
- Routine
- Reward

Step 7: If possible, create a routine loop for each habit within the stack

While each habit has a loop, you need not have a loop for each habit if a stack loop can cover the same. Also, in cases where habits in a stack share the same items in the loop, there is no need for repetition. However, those habits that have unique items in a loop or are so different from the rest in a stack, then, you can let them have their unique loop.

So far, in this Section, we have dealt with steps (1) and (2). Steps (3) to (7) will be performed in each mentioned stack in subsequent Sections.

Killing the bad habits

Just as you are capable of creating bad habits, you too are capable of killing your bad habits. The following are ways by which you can kill your bad habits;

1. Strengthen your willpower
2. Boost your self-awareness
3. Gather emotional support
4. Engage in sublimation
5. Practice substitution
6. Create and implement habit stacks

Strengthen your Willpower

Will is related to desire. If you do not want something very much, then the will to succeed is likely to be weak.

Desire can be good or bad depending on what we want to achieve. If you want to achieve the best of you, then, you should prop up good desire as this will be the fuel that will propel your willpower.

Boost your Self-Awareness

Self-Awareness refers to conscious knowledge of one's own character, feelings, motives, and desires. To be self-aware is to learn and discover who you are. By discovering who you are, you are able to establish your sense of purpose and use your willpower to pursue it to the highest possible end.

Gather Emotional Support

Bad habits die hard. Hiding them from your trusted friend(s) and family may not help much. The easiest way to fight bad habits is to gather emotional support from your trusted family members and friends. They will offer you advice, understand your plight and encourage you to overcome them. They could even go further to offer you a reward for your success. This also makes it hard for you to revert to your bad behavior since you will not just want to fail yourself but also you will not want to fail your loved ones.

Engage in Sublimation

Sublimation involves replacing a primitive urge with a more creative one. For example, if you feel desire to binge eat, you may replace your desire with playing piano or playing tennis. Thus, you haven't really satisfied your primitive urge, but you have suppressed it by replacing it with a more creative urge for piano. Thus, sublimation is about replacing one urge with another urge but not providing an alternative means to satisfying the urge.

Practice Substitution

Substitution is about finding a better alternative that satisfies the same urge. For example, if you are an alcoholic, you may overcome addiction to alcohol by participating in tea parties rather than alcohol parties. This will serve your urge to 'drink and socialize' but by substituting alcohol for tea. Thus, in substitution you don't suppress the urge, but find a better means of satisfying it.

Create habit stacks

Through habit stacking, you are able to easily kill bad habits and enhance good habits.

HABIT STACKING FOR HOME LIFE

Home is from where we wake up most of our life. It is from where get up to work or study. It is where we have our family. It is also where we retire to rest after a busy day. Yet, there are those who are happy to be at home while others are not. The difference is mainly due to the home environment.

Habits play a great role in determining the kind of home environment one has. You can have a good home environment or a bad home environment depending on your home life habits.

Bad home habits to kill

The following are bad home habits to kill.

1. Poor kitchen habits
2. Poor bathroom habits
3. Poor laundry habits
4. Poor dining habits
5. Poor bedroom habits

Poor kitchen habits

Bad kitchen habits may lead to food contamination and germ infection which may cause stomach upsets and food poisoning.

These bad habits include:

1. Not washing dishes on time
2. Not arranging your dishes after washing
3. Pilling refuse in the kitchen

Poor bathroom habits

Poor bathroom habits may lead to poor hygiene leading to spread of infections such as skin fungi and bacterial infections. They may also cause strained relations amongst family members or bathtub users.

Such poor habits include;

1. Overstaying while others are waiting to use it
2. Not cleaning your bathtub and sinks after using them
3. Leaving your underwear in the bathroom

Poor laundry habits

Poor laundry habits may not only lead to poor grooming and social isolation as one gets shunned by friends but may also cause psychological problems such as low self-esteem. They may also lead to parasitic infections such as lice, mites and bedbugs and skin infections.

Such habits include:

1. Not ironing your clothes immediately after removing from the drier
2. Piling your dirty clothes with clean ones
3. Soaking your clothes without sorting them out

Poor dining habits

Poor dining habits can lead one to be shunned by others or regarded with low esteem in social places.

Such habits include:

1. Talking while eating
2. Eating from the bedroom
3. Staring at a guest's mouth while eating
4. Gouging
5. Not removing used utensils from dining table after eating
6. Not wiping dining table after using it

Poor bedroom habits

Poor bedroom habits can cause you loss of sleep, stress and even frustration. Poor bedroom habits have been known to cause strained relations between married couples. This could lead to divorce.

These bad habits include:

1. Having sleep distractions in your bedroom
2. Sleeping late
3. Waking up late
4. Snoozing the alarm
5. Not spreading your bed after waking up
6. Putting your combs, mirrors, makeup tubes and other beauty paraphernalia on your bed
7. Cluttering your bedroom

Good hygiene habits

It is commonly said that cleanliness is next to Godliness. This is so true in the sense that, if you have to keep the best of your Godly being, then, you have to be clean. Poor hygiene is the primary cause of many germ infections. Outbreaks of cholera, typhoid and dysentery are often caused by poor hygiene. Most stomach upsets are due to poor hygiene.

Good bathroom habits

1. Be punctual in using shared bathroom in the house during morning and evening hours
2. Clean the bathroom after use and leave it dry
3. Get out your inner wears with you.

Good laundry habits

1. Keep your dirty clothes in a dirty cloth bin
2. Iron your clothes immediately after removing from the dry line
3. Sort your clothes prior to soaking
4. Don't soak your clothes for long hours

Good dining habits

1. Eat in silence and chew while your mouth is shut
2. Eat from the dining room
3. Keep your eyes off your guest's mouth while eating
4. Drinking water and other fluids without galloping

5. Remove utensils from the dining table after use
6. Clean the dining table immediately after use

Good bedroom habits

1. Remove all sleep distractions from your bedroom e.g. noise, powerful light, etc.
2. Sleep early in the night, at least by 10 p.m. if you nedd to wake up by 6 a.m. This will grant you ample time to sleep.
3. Wake up early from bed so as to avoid getting to work or school late, feeling tired during the day and reduce the risk of headaches and body aches.
4. Spread your bed immediately after waking up.
5. Don't clutter your bedroom by making it another kind of store.

STACKING THE GOOD HOME LIFE HABITS

Trigger: Alarm Clock

Routine:

1. Wake up early in the morning

2. Spread your bed immediately

3. Wash your face (health stack)

4. Brush your teeth (health stack)

5. Carry out morning workouts (health stack)

6. Go bathe

7. Clean and tidy bathroom after bathing

8. Get to dining table and have your breakfast

9. Clear and wipe your dining table after eating breakfast

10. Check HEALTH STACK for what you need to do while at home

11. Check RELATIONSHIP STACK for what you need to do while at home

Reward: Munch some carrot stick as you head off to work or study

HABIT STACKING FOR HEALTH

Health is wealth. You cannot be successful if you are not healthy. There is nothing worth achieving if you have to sacrifice your health for it. Unfortunately, many have engaged in bad health habits that have caused them diseases, unhealthy medical conditions and even deaths.

Health habits are important for one to maintain optimal health. This helps one to lead a healthy, happy and fulfilling life.

Bad health habits

These are habits that compromise one's health. Bad health habits include;

1. Poor hygiene habits
2. Poor diet habits
3. Poor activity habits

Poor hygiene habits

Poor hygiene is one of the primary causes of disease and poor health. The following are some of the poor hygiene habits;

1. Not brushing your teeth as expected

2. Not bathing every morning

3. Wearing clothes more than once

Poor diet habits

Poor diet habits have increasing become common. Poor diet compromises your health by denying your body required nutrients and adding unwanted toxins.

Some of the common poor diet habits include:

- Bingeing – overindulgence in eating
- Taking CRAP (Carbonated, Refined, Alcoholic and Processed) foods
- Avoiding cooking own meals
- Substituting drinking water with beverages

Poor activity habits

Sedentary life is characterized by lack of activity. Our body was made to be on the move most of the time. However, due to challenges of modernity, we find ourselves spending lots of time behind work or study desk.

Nonetheless, there are certain habits that we have accustomed ourselves to that makes this situation much worse. Such poor activity habits include;

- Spending most of your free time watching movies and playing video games
- Spending most of your free time on social media networks
- Not doing fitness workouts
- Not carrying out simple manual house chores such as lawn mowing, cleaning the house, washing dishes, etc.

Good health habits

To be able to overcome bad health habits, we need to create have positive habits so that they can fill the void created by killing bad habits.

Good hygiene habits

1. Wash your face
2. Brush your teeth
3. Bath after workouts

Good diet habits

1. Stock foodstuff ingredients so that you don't fall victim of quick fixes in the form of toxic fast foods in restaurants.

2. Take breakfast every day morning after shower. Ensure that the breakfast has balanced diet.

3. Avoid eating when not hungry or under the influence of cravings

4. Avoid taking CRAP (Carbonated, Refined, Alcoholic and Processed) foods

5. Cook your own meals. Pack some for your lunch while at work or school

6. Take water after eating and when thirsty. Avoid substituting water with beverages, more so, soft drinks.

7. Practice clean eating, that is, eating food as close to natural as possible.

8. Avoid bad sugars (added sugar and simple carbohydrates)

9. Take at least three meals a day.

10. Take meals in small portions, more frequently as opposed to large portions less frequently

Good activity habits

Your body needs mobility exercises to remain in good form. This is how it was designed to be. It wasn't designed to remain seated or standing for long hours.

The following are good activity habits:

1. Carrying out some workouts immediately after washing your face and brushing your teeth early in the morning after waking up.
2. Taking short-breaks, at least after every hours, from seating while in office or study room to walk around, pick a file from the cabinet are converse with a colleague
3. Stretching your limbs frequently while seated
4. Standing up straight frequently (at least after every 45 minutes, or so for a minute)
5. Having lunch-time light exercises such as taking a walk, doing press-ups, yoga, etc.
6. Having evening workouts after work or study
7. Spending at least 3 hours of workouts over the weekend, possibly per day, if you are free on both days.
8. Carrying out household and homestead chores while free instead of hiring someone else to do. Cutting grass,

mowing, pruning, sweep compound, cleaning, washing, etc, helps to enhance your physical activity. They are the best things you can easily do without even realizing that you are carrying out some form of workout.

STACKING THE GOOD HEALTH HABITS

Trigger: Checklist / To Do List

Routine:

What you need to do at home:

1. Check your kitchen store for food ingredients that need to be bought and list them down to buy later in the day

2. Do common household chores while free at home

What you need to do at work/study:

3. Punctually arrive at your study/work station

4. Implement RELATIONSHIP HABITS that you need to perform at work and implement them. These include greetings, pep talk, etc (see next Section on Habit Stack for Relationships)

5. Take short breaks (5 minutes) after every one hour from your office or study desk – do walk around in the room, walk to the next room/office, go to the lavatory, etc.

6. Stand up one in a while to stretch your limbs and back

7. Have lunch packed lunch from home

8. Do some yoga or press-ups during your lunch-time

    After work/study:

9. Do some workout exercises, possibly outdoor fitness workouts

Reward: Give yourself a treat of natural healthy balanced dinner diet you have never eaten before. Play an outdoor physical game with your family, friends or workmates.

HABIT STACK FOR RELATIONSHIPS

Relationships are important for our overall wellbeing. Without good relationships, we end up stressed, unhappy and more susceptible to diseases, negative emotions, mental disease and even suicide. Relationships are what develop us as human beings. Relationships help us build our careers, families and achieve our lifelong goals.

Bad relationship habits

There are certain habits that cause poor relationships. Such bad relationship habits include;

1. Poor parenting habits
2. Poor partner relationship habits
3. Poor social habits

Poor parenting habits

Poor parenting habits often leads to deviant behaviors in children, child's poor emotional and social development leading to such children becoming social delinquents. Some of these habits include;

1. Failure to discipline children when they persistently go wrong
2. Failure to set acceptable behavioral limits
3. Failing to set activity limits
4. Consistently giving in to your kid
5. Acting like a servant
6. Using intimidation
7. Being a buddy before being a parent
8. Comparing and criticizing
9. Overdoing good gestures
10. Not listening enough

Poor spousal relationship

1. Maintaining relationship scorecard – A relationship should be free and ever-fresh for it to succeed. Keeping records of other's failures would make it hard to forgive. Without forgiveness, relationship cannot be healthy.
2. Dropping 'hints' and other passive aggressions – Dropping 'hints' makes the other person in your relationship feel

that you are not open enough. This can hurt the relationship as your partner feels that you are hiding something. If you are displeased, just open up and tell it frankly.

3. Holding the relationship hostage – Holding relationship hostage is basing your relationship on certain conditions without which you deem your relationship non-existent. For example, basing your relationship on the amount of gifts or favors you receive is making it hostage. This is known to cause animosity as one party feels exploited.

4. Blaming your partner for your own emotions – Blaming your partner for your emotions is likely going to make your partner feel that you are selfish and irresponsible while at the same time making you not seek solutions to your emotional problems.

5. Buying solutions for relationship's problems – When your partner feels disappointed, the most important thing is to go to the root of the problem rather than covering it with gifts. Doing so buries the problem rather than solving them thus bringing discontentment.

Poor social relationship habits

1. Seeking attention by complaining – this is going to be considered as nagging and lack of appreciation. It may result into you being shunned or isolated.

2. Focusing on your inner monologue instead of dialogue in front of you – engaging in dialogue only comes from attentive listening. Focusing on your inner self-talk rather than engaging with others may cause them to think that you are an aloof person.

3. Multi-tasking while you chat – This may make the person you are chatting with consider you disrespectful and disinterested in the chat.

4. Not paying attention to the people you care about most – Social relationships need attention. Without giving due attention to people you care about most may lead to them feeling neglected and thus build resentment.

5. Constantly fishing for compliments – Wait for compliments to come on their own in the most natural way. Overtly seeking compliments may lower your integrity.

Good relationship habits

Just as bad habits, the following are key categories of good habits:

1. Good parenting habits
2. Good spousal habits
3. Good social habits

Good parenting habits

1. Correcting and disciplining your kids.
2. Spending more time with your kids.
3. Not compensating your kids for household chores.

Good spousal habits

1. Write-off any record of wrongdoing from your memory.
2. Practicing honesty and transparency for wrongs done.
3. Freeing your spouse to make independent decisions.
4. Taking responsibility for own emotions.
5. Dealing with spousal problems by digging up to the root cause.

Good social habits

1. Stop complaining all the time.
2. Listening to others instead of own self-talk while engaging them.
3. Giving full attention to others while engaging them .

4. Paying keen attention to loved ones.

5. Avoid seeking compliments.

STACKING GOOD HABITS FOR RELATIONSHIPS

Environment: Home

Cue: Playful kids

Role: Parent

Routine:

1. Greet your kids
2. Help them have meals
3. Drop them to school (if school day)
4. Pick them up from school (if school day)
5. Play with them (after school, if school day)
6. Correct where they go wrong
7. Discipline them when they do bad manners

Reward: Enjoying some good play with kids; listen to kid's stories.

Environment: Home

Cue: Spouse presence

Role: Spouse

Routine:

1. Hug and kiss your spouse

Carry out home life habits

2. Have dinner together (with kids, if you have)
3. Share out household chores

Carry out health habits together

4. Go jogging together
5. Attend gym together

Reward: Anniversary gifts, surprise gift, pleasantries

Environment: Work

Cue: Work mates

Role: Co-worker

Routine

1. Make a greeting handshake with your co-worker
2. Share out common tasks
3. Share break time conversation
4. Play some game together

Reward: Gifts and pleasantries

Environment: Study

Cue: Presence of your study mate

Role: Co-student

Routine

1. Make a greeting handshake with your co-student, if possible, a hug
2. Talk about your previous studies
3. Talk about what you expect for the day
4. Share break time conversation
5. Share out a meal
6. Play together

Reward: Share out an outing with your loved ones in a new unique place.

HABIT STACKS FOR FINANCES

Finance is the core of personal freedom. Finances determine whether you will exist as an independent person or you will become dependent on others.

Financial freedom is the best guarantee of your very own individuality. If you are not financially free, then, you will be forced to suppress your own individuality for the sake of others. This can degrade your self-esteem thus causing lack of self-confidence in life. Mental and psychological consequences of financial problems can be devastating.

Poor financial habits can wreck you no matter how much you earn. Those who grow their finances and make good investments are not necessarily those who earn high but those who have good financial habits.

Before we have a take on good financial habits, let's discuss poor financial habits that we need to get rid off so that good financial habits can occupy the freed space.

Poor finance habits

The following are some of the poor financial habits that you need to banish in your habit stack for finances:

1. Spending more than you earn
2. Not saving out of your earnings
3. Impulse buying
4. Making quick poorly-thought-out and poorly-researched investment decisions

Good finance habits

The following are good financial habits that you ought to engender as part of your habit stack for finances;

1. Spend within your means
2. Save at least one-third of your earnings
3. Plan your purchases
4. Take time to make investment decisions

Tools to enable you manage your finance habits

The good thing about finance is that it has plenty of tools that can enable you to manage your finance habits.

The following are some of these important tools;

1. Financial Plan
2. Budget
3. Charts

Financial Plan

This is plan on what you want to achieve with your money. For example, you may want to buy a car, buy a house, start a business, etc. All these are what you want to do. They are also your expenditures. However, they are not normal daily expenditures such as buying foodstuff, toiletries and other consumables. These are long-term capital expenditures. To be able to achieve your capital expenditures, you will need to have savings. If savings are not enough, or if urgency is supreme, then, you would probably take a loan. However, loan is a liability. Loan enables you to consume your future income today. You must not forget this.

Though beyond the scope of this book, a simple plan needs to incorporate the following;

- Vision – The grander picture of where you want to be

- Mission – The reason as to why you want to achieve your vision
- Goal – A state of achieving your mission
- Objectives – A set of targets required to achieve your goal
- Execution – Implementing your objectives.

Kindly get more acquaintance on FINANCIAL PLANNING from Business and Finance books.

Budget

A budget is simply a forecast of your projected expenditure and source of income to achieve the expenditure.

A budget is the most effective financial control tool.

A budget helps you to:

1. Allocate your income
2. Control you expenditure
3. Stick to your commitments
4. Take appropriate steps to stay within your means

There is more to do with budgeting that is beyond the scope of this book. Kindly get more acquaintance on with BUDGETING from Business and Finance books.

Charts

Charts are simply pictorial representation of your financial data so as to derive more meaningful information.

- When you make a trend chart of your expenditure, you are easily alerted when your expenditure goes up more than expected. This triggers a quicker action than would have otherwise been if you were just reading your records.

- Pie chart is a good chart, especially for your household expenditure. A pie chart shows how items are competing to have a share of your income pie. It such easy to digest.

- Bar charts can help you comparatively visualize the height or length of 'chocolate' bars that have consumed your expenditure.

There are many ways to use your chart. Though commonly used to reflect your domestic expenditure, they can also be relevant if you have multiple sources of income such as multiple jobs so as to compare which one contributes more to your needs, etc.

The best way to come up with charts is to tabulate your data on spreadsheet software such as **MS EXCEL** or **GOOGLE SHEETS** and quickly derive a chart that automatically updates whenever you add or alter data.

It is important that make a habit of drawing charts to represent your financial information.

Further details on Charts are beyond the scope of this book. Kindly get more acquaintance on with CHARTS from BASIC STATISTICS books.

STACKING GOOD HABITS FOR FINANCES

Cue: Income / daily expenditure

Routine

1. Plan what you want to do with your income and keep on refining your plan
2. Make budget of your income and expenditure and keep on updating your budget
3. Draw appropriate charts to get more informative visual representation of your performance
4. Make purchase and expenditure decisions based on your budget
5. Review your plan and budget and make appropriate corrective and control actions

Reward: Buy yourself something worth remembering from the savings you would have otherwise lost had you surrendered to the pressure of an impulse buying urge that would have violated your budget.

HABIT STACKS FOR BUSINESS

Business is such a complex entity, no matter how small or big it is. There are certain habits that will make your business succeed or fail. These habits fall into the following main categories;

1. Poor work habits
2. Poor leadership habits
3. Poor customer care habits

Bad habits at work

Bad habits at work not only lowers your productivity and frustrates your career progression, but they do also affect your co-workers and deny your employer maximum opportunity for growth.

The following are some of the bad habits at work that you must eliminate through habit stack for business:

1. Not being punctual – Arriving late at work not only steals your employer's time but also inconveniences others that you are supposed to work with as a team.
2. Isolating yourself – Most workplaces require team-players in order for work to flow smoothly. Isolating

yourself from others obstructs this smooth flow of work thus impairing productivity at workplace.

3. Avoiding Work – Avoiding work not only denies your employer the much-needed labor but also denies you the opportunity to optimize on your experience.

4. Resisting Change – Change is inevitable and the only think that enables an organization to perpetually survive. Resisting change may lead you to risk your long-term employability as neither your job nor your organization can survive in the long-run without change.

5. Being Negative – Being negative results in poor relationship between you and your colleagues or your supervisors/juniors. This may cause low work morale resulting into low productivity.

6. Gossiping – Gossiping is a sign of inferiority complex. Gossiping is mostly fueled by jealousy. Gossiping may destroy work relationships thus resulting into enmity at work which may cause negative conflicts.

7. Procrastinating, then rushing – This is an erratic behavior characteristic of psychological instability. You work within a system. Thus, if you can't go with the pace in the work system, you end up disrupting the

normal flow of work thus resulting into the work system's overall sub-optimality.

Bad leadership habits

Leadership is what navigates the firm's direction in the murky world of business competition. Good leadership not only make a firm survive, but prosper to greater heights of success.

However, bad leadership habits can not only hamper your leadership abilities but can also collapse a firm entrusted to your leadership care.

The following are some of the bad leadership habits that you ought to banish using habit stack for business;

1. Finding problems in everything – Being critical is important. But as a leader, it should be measured and prudent. Otherwise, those who follow you may feel unwanted and thus give up.

2. Never providing a positive praise – Lack of positive praise may be interpreted by many as a subtle sign of dissatisfaction or lack of recognition for others efforts. This may lead to resentment.

3. Struggling to make decisions – There is nothing that is as bad in leadership as being indecisive. Struggling to make decisions is a sign of indecisiveness. This may send signals that you are a weak leader and thus prompt your replacement.

4. Failing to pay attention to the works of the people who are working for you – Paying attention to what others are doing on your behalf is a good sign of being caring and appreciative. Failure to provide attention to what is being done for you may lead to low morale of those doing it.

5. Changing direction without informing other people that you have changed direction – Leadership is about forthrightness. People follow your direction. When you change direction without notice, this breeds distrust amongst your followers as they may consider you treacherous.

Bad customer care habits

Customer care is the core of every business success. Customers are the revenue source of your business. Thus, how you handle them will determine how your revenue flows.

The following are some of the poor customer-care habits;

1. Not facing customers as you attend them

2. Expressing negative body language

3. Faking out a smile

4. Talking to colleagues or on phone while attending to a customer

5. Expressing negative emotions as sign of displeasure by a customer

Good habits at work

1. Being always punctual
2. Engaging the company of co-workers
3. Being ever ready to take up new assignments
4. Embracing a positive change attitude
5. Being positive and optimistic
6. Avoid gossiping
7. Avoid procrastination

Good leadership habits

1. Finding solutions in everything
2. Positively praising good deeds
3. Embracing decision-making
4. Paying keen attention to the work of others
5. Informing others about change of direction

Good customer care habits

1. Engaging eye contact with customers as you engage them

2. Expressive positive body language
3. Having a genuine smile
4. Stopping phone conversation while attending to a customer
5. Avoiding negative emotions as a means of showing displeasure

STACKING GOOD HABITS FOR BUSINESS

Cue: Clock

Task: Report to work

Routine

1. Report to your workstation
2. Employ relevant **Relationship routines** from the RELATIONSHIPS STACK
3. Review and update your work schedule/diary
4. Start performing your first task on schedule
5. Follow your work schedule to the end.

6. Intervene where necessary to implement **Health routines** relevant to work from the HEALTH STACK

Reward: Take a break to rest whenever a given task is accomplished

Cue: Leadership plan

Task: Leading

Routine:

1. Review and update your Leadership plan for the day
2. Review and update your diary and journal
3. Review and update yourself on relevant **Relationship routines** from the RELATIONSHIPS STACK
4. Make enquiries and receive updates on assigned tasks
5. Assign new tasks and/or instructions based on the feedback of your inquiries
6. Motivate and inspire your staff performance
7. Intervene where necessary to implement **Health routines** relevant to work from the HEALTH STACK

8. Engage other key stakeholders relevant to your leadership e.g. clients, partners, associates, mentors, advisors, etc.

9. Receive and review reports on work-in-progress and task completion reports

10. Take appropriate corrective or supportive action based on the review of reports presented

11. Reward success.

Reward: Celebrate with your respective staff or workmates for each assignment successfully achieved.

CONCLUSION

Thank you for reading this book, "Habit Stacking: Introduce Small Habits into Your Routine to Beat Procrastination and Double Your Output".

It is my sincere hope that this book has enabled you to easily and practically infuse good habits into your daily life in small, yet powerful doses of routine. I also hope these routines have been able to help you overcome procrastination and eventual double your output.

Please share your lessons learned from this book with others. More so, encourage them to acquire this book as their daily companion in their battle to fight bad habits and save themselves from the monstrous time disaster – procrastination.

Thank you!

The end… almost!

Reviews are not easy to come by.

As an independent author with a tiny marketing budget, I rely on readers, like you, to leave a short review on Amazon.

Even if it's just a sentence or two!

So if you enjoyed the book, please head to the product page, and leave a review as shown below.

I am very appreciative for your review as it truly makes a difference. Thank you from the bottom of my heart for purchasing this book and reading it to the end.

Good luck!

www.ingramcontent.com/pod-product-compliance
Lightning Source LLC
Chambersburg PA
CBHW071025080526
44587CB00015B/2508